GOD WILL GIVE YOU

EVERYTHING

YOU REQUIRE TO

ACCOMPLISH

YOUR GOALS

IF YOU HAVE FAITH

Geraldine Smith

Copyright © 2024 Geraldine Smith

First Edition

PAGE PUBLISHING
Conneaut Lake, PA

First originally published by Page Publishing 2024

ISBN 979-8-89157-918-7 (pbk)
ISBN 979-8-89157-935-4 (digital)

Printed in the United States of America

Prayer is a bridge that closes the gap between
us and a source that enables a relationship that
transforms our experiences of self and God.
Prayer is a request for God to intervene in our daily lives.

CONTENTS

B I B L E

This book a source of information about Scriptures never spoken of or discussed that brings hope, faith, and love. The Bible offers so much.

The Bible is the greatest book ever written.

Every scripture is ordained by God.

Always remember that the Bible is God's infallible divine inspired Word.

The Bible was written over 1,500 generations by different men.

The Bible can never be the private and excusive property on one religion.

However, many religion added their own "how believers go about their religion—what is, what is not." Your evidence must be manifested in the Bible. The Bible is your proof. Never argue your point without scripture for proof.

If you cannot come to an agreement, walk away. Always be strong in your convictions in grace that is in Jesus. However, you must interpret the Bible according to the content of the verse.

Always read a few verses preceding and immediately following the verse you are focusing on.

Each book has a specific purpose to bring a special message.

The Bible is a book of diverse instructions and interpretations.

The Bible offers

1. instructions,
2. comfort,
3. guidance in perplexity,
4. discernment, and
5. compassion.

It gives advice on how to handle

1. stress,
2. sorrows,
3. discomfort,
4. problems, and
5. rebuke for sin.

PASSAGES THAT DISCUSS THEM

A. Forms of Government
Citizenship under the Theocracy
God was the direct ruler of His people (Exodus 19:3–8)

1. Criminal laws
Crimes against the Public
Bribery (Deuteronomy 16:19, Judges 16:5, Job 15:34, Proverbs 17:23)
2. Contempt for the law
3. Perjury
4. Preventing or obstruction
5. Treason

Things That Concerned Jesus

I.   Commission: "Go ye therefore teaching them all things what God command" (Matthew 28:19).

II. Compassion: This was the heartbeat of Jesus's ministry healing.

III. Concern: Jesus was always concerned about people's needs. Jesus saw a moral obligation toward each other (Colossians 1:3, Psalm 106:23, Luke 19:41, Acts 20:30).

IV. Intercession: Jesus interceded for us when He gave His life for us on the cross.

V.   Contact: It begins with a personal relationship with Jesus. A love for Christ produces a love for mankind

VI. Tact: This suggests sensitivity toward others' feelings. There are times we must ask God for wisdom and lean not unto our own understanding (James 1:5). Be natural, be courteous, and be a good listener. You never know what a person is going through.

Steps to a Christian Life:

1. Repent (Luke 13:3).

2. Receive Him. You need the Savior (John 1:12).

3. Regeneration follow: This is what Christ does for you. A miracle of spiritual life performed by the Holy Ghost, not the will of man but of God (John 1:13). See also John 11:25.

4. Rejoice publicly – Make your testimony for Christ: "For with the heart man believeth unto righteousness; and with the mouth confession to made unto salvation" (Romans 10:9–10, Matthew 10:32–33).

5. Request a water baptism – "He that believeth and is baptized shall be saved: but he that believeth not shall be damned" (Mark 16:16).

6. Read the Bible.

7. Resist the devil – Temptation is not sin. It is yielding to temptation that is sin.

8. Restitution – Your guilt is gone, and you can convert your influence for good: "If I have taken anything from any man by false accusations I restore him four fold" (Luke 19:8).

EXCUSES

1. "I am my own boss."

   "Why is God so hard?"

2. It is not God who is hard. It is you (Romans 2:25).

3. "I am religious—I go to church. I pay my tithe." Religion is often on the outside.

4. "I am trying to be a Christian." It is not trying to be a Christian. It is trusting that counts. Jehovah is my strength and my song. He is my salvation (Isaiah 12:2).

5. "What is sin?"

   a. Sin is breaking God's law (1 John 3:10).

   b. Everything that is not morally right is sin (1 John 5:17).

   c. Unbelief is sin (1 John 6:8–9).

   d. Questionable indulgences is sin (Romans 4:23).

   e. Undone duty is a sin (James 4:17).

6. "My sins are small. Why should I have to worry?"
   One should worry because any sin torments.
   "There is no peace, said the Lord, unto the wicked"
   (Isaiah 48:22).

Things in Our Lives

We often complicate life.

1. If you miss somebody, call them.
2. If you want to meet, invite them.
3. If you have a question, ask.
4. If you don't like something, say it.
5. If you love someone, tell them.
6. Be honest.

Emergency Help

1. Upset?   Read John 14.
2. Weak?   Read Psalm 18:1–29.
3. Lonely?   Read Psalm 23.
4. Sinned?   Read Psalm 51.
5. Worried?   Read Matthew 8:19–31.
6. Anxious?   Read Philippians 4:4–9.
7. Unhappy?   Read Colossians 3:12–17.
8. Depressed?   Read Psalm 27.
9. In danger?   Read Psalm 23.
10. Lack of faith?   Read Exodus.
11. Need courage?   Read Joshua.
12. Need direction?   Read Psalm 73:21–26
13. Seeking peace?   Read Matthew 11:25–30.
14. Struggling with loss?   Read Luke 15.
15. Struggling financially?   Read Psalm 37.
16. Discouraged with work?   Read Psalm 126.

SIN ENSLAVES

Sin enslaves you with hate, jealousy, and greed for money and power (John 8:34).

Why does God allow evil in the world? God gave us free choice. Freedom of choice is the greatest gift to all men on earth. Sin originated in man, not in God (Romans 6:14).

Seven Deadly Sins (Proverbs 6:16–19)

1. A proud look
2. A lying tongue and hands that shed innocent blood
3. A false witness that speaks lies
4. Soweth discord among brethren
5. A heart that deviseth wicked imagination
6. Feet running to mischief
7. Iniquity, the depth of sin, setting out to hurt and harm someone

There are other sins, stealing, making excuses to get out of trouble, etc.

The number is defined as complete, the end, done, finished.

1. Jacob's seven years for Rachel (Genesis 29:20, 27).
2. Bowed – "And he passed over before them; and bow himself down to the ground (7) times until he came near to his brother" (Genesis 33:3).
3. Mourning – "They mourned with a great and very sore lamentation: and he made a mourning for his father seven days (Genesis 50:10).
4. Wedding feast – A riddle (7) seven days to find out.
5. Fasting – And all the men of the stayed until on the (7) seventh day (1 Samuel).
6. And God blessed the (7) seventh day (Genesis 2:3).
7. Seven (7) days in a week.
8. Leviticus spoke to the children of Israel saying (In the seventh month). Chapters 23–24

9. Seven colors in the rainbow. Genesis, 9, 10

10. Seven (7) wicked spirits – "Then goeth he, and himself seven other spirits more wicked than himself, and they enter in and dwell there; and the man is worse than the first" (Matthew 12:45).

11. Seven (7) churches – Revelation 1:4.

12. Passover – Seven (7) days shall ye eat unleavened bread (Exodus 12:15).

13. Joseph the Dreamer – Seven lean years, seven fat years. Gensis 37–44

14. Miracles, plagues, Jericho falls. Joshua 5–6

15. Joshua went around the wall 7 (seven) times.

16. Seven loaves, seven baskets (Matthew 15:37).

17. Symbols of Purification – "The words of the Lord are pure words…purified (7) times" (Psalm 12:6).

18. Plagues – And the (7) seven angels came out the temple (Revelation 15:6).

SEVEN RULES TO LIVE BY

Seven rules to live by:

1. Let it go.
2. Ignore.
3. Give it time.
4. Don't compare.
5. Stay calm.
6. It's on you.
7. Smile.

SEVEN (7) SAYINGS FROM THE CROSS

"Father forgive them For they know not what they do" (Luke 23:34).
       1 2   3   4 5   6 7

"Thou shall be with me in Paradise, said Jesus" (Luke 23:43).
  1   2 3 4 5 6 7

"(My God) (My God) Why hath thou forsaken me?" (Matthew 27:46).
   1   2   3 4 5 6   7

"Father into thy hands, I commend my spirit."

SEVEN BLESSINGS
DECLARED BY JESUS

The Beatitudes – 7 Blessings

1. Blessed are the poor in spirit for theirs is the kingdom of heaven.
2. Blessed are the that mourn: for they shall be comfort.
3. Blessed are the meek: for they shall inherit the earth.
4. Blessed are they which do hunger and thirst after righteousness for the shall be filled.
5. Blessed are the merciful for they shall obtain mercy.
6. Blessed are the pure in heart, for they shall see God.
7. Blessed are the peacemakers; for they shall be called the children of God.

Dynamic Doctrines

1. Man's Universal Guilt   Romans 1:18, 2:18
2. Atonement   Romans 5
3. The New Birth   John 3
4. Justification of Faith   Ephesians 2:1–16
5. Christ the Good Shepherd   John 10–18
6. Christ's Humiliation and Exaltation   Philippians 2:5–11
7. Resurrections of the Dead   1 Thessalonians 4:13–18
8. Second coming of Christ   2 Thessalonians 1:7, 2:2
9. The New Heaven and New Earth   Revelation 21:22

SEVEN (7) REQUESTS TO GOD
(THE LORD'S PRAYER)

1. Give us this day
2. Give us our daily bread
3. Forgive us our debts
4. Lead us not into temptation
5. Deliver us from evil
6. As we forgive our debts
7. They kingdom come unto me with power and glory forever

FOR WITH GOD, ALL
THINGS ARE POSSIBLE.

With man this is impossible, but with God, all things are possible (Matthew 19:26).

Throughout the Bible, God's people accomplished unfathomable tasks. God is most glorified by bringing an event to pass which seems impossible. With God, there is always hope, no matter how bad thing seems impossible. His power makes all things possible. You must believe.

Steps to Christian Life

1. Read your Bible daily
2. Learn the secret of prayer
3. Rely constantly on the Holy Spirit
4. Attend church regularly
5. Be a witnessing Christian
6. Let love be the ruling principle of your life
7. Love thy neighbor as thy self
8. Be an obedient Christian
9. Learn how to avoid temptation

Dr. Wilbur M. Smith gives us seven (7) great things that the Bible let us know the following:

All have sinned and come short of glory of God.

1. The Bible discovers and convicts us of sin.
2. The Bible cleans us from the pollutions of sin.
3. The Bible imparts our strength.
4. The Bible instructs us in what to do.
5. The Bible provides us with a sword for victory over sin.
6. The Bible makes our life fruitful.
7. The Bible gives us power to pray.

PRAYER

1. Prayer is usually a communication with God.
2. Prayer is a bridge that closes the gap between us and our source that enables a relationship that transforms our experience of self and of God.
3. Prayer is a request for God to intervene in our daily lives.
4. Prayer is an opening. It changes the one who prays. It changes the status quo of the person's inferior life.
5. Prayer is an admission of need. It is a divine intervention.

When reading the Bible, do the following:

1. Reflect, meditate, reread the verse.
2. Ponder who is speaking and about whom the passage is speaking.
3. Consider goodness and greatness.
4. Dwell in your thought deeply.

5. Let the Word of God be meaningful and real unto you.
6. Take time to think and meditate.
7. Let the Holy Spirit guide your mind.

Spiritual Standards

The Sermon on the mount   Matthew 5–7
The Golden Rule   Matthew 7:12
The Greatest Commandment   Matthew 22–36–40
The Righteousness of Faith   Romans 3:19–28
The Royal Law   Romans 13:8–10
Christ's New Commandment   John 13:34–35
                               1 Corinthians 13

PRACTICAL PRECEPTS

1. Christian Fruitiness   John 15
2. Christians Responsibilities   Romans 12 and 13
3. Christian Stewardship   2 Corinthians 8 and 9
4. Re vailing Prayer   Matthew 6:5–15
      Philippians 4:6–7

Seven Rules of Life
The Lord Hates

Seven rules of life

1. Let go – Never ruin a good day by things of a bad day
2. Ignore – Don't listen to lies _ hear say
   They said – who are they
3. Don't except lies as truth whom you know it is a lie
4. Don't compare
5. Stay calm
6. You are in charge
7. Smile – Life is short

Psalms 23

The Lord is my shepherd;

I shall not want.

He makes me to lie down in green pastures:

He leads me beside the still waters.

He restores my soul; he leads me in path of righteousness for his name's sake.

Yea, though I walk through shadow of death, I will fear no evil; for thou are with me; you prepared a table before me in the presence of my enemies; you anoint my head with oil; my cup runs over, surely goodness and mercy shall follow me all the days of my life; and I will dwell in the house of the Lord forever.

Seven (7) Ways To Live A Good Life

1. Always be honest – Proverbs 12:22
2. Forgive and forget – Micah 7:18
3. Be kindhearted – Ephesians 4:32
4. Keep your promises – Romans 4:21
5. Work hard – Colossians 3:23
6. Be thankful – Thessalonians 5:18
7. Never give up – Philippians 4:13

SCRIPTURES THAT AFFECT OUR LIVES AND OTHERS'

1. Actions — Matthew 12:33, 35
2. Adultery — Matthew 5:28
3. Affections — Matthew 15:18–20
4. Desire — Roman 10:1
5. Doubt — Mark 11:23
6. Fear — Isaiah 33:4
7. Hatred — Leviticus 19:17
8. Joy — Acts 2:26
9. Love — Mark 12:30, 33
10. Lust — Romans 1:22
11. Meditation — Psalm 19:14
12. Mischief — Psalm 28:3
13. Obedience — Roman 6:17
14. Presumption — Esther 7:7
15. Pride — Proverbs 16:5
16. Purpose — 2 Corinthians 9:7
17. Reason — Mark 2:28
18. Rebellion — Jeremiah 5:23
19. Sorrow — John 14:1
20. Thought — Matthew 9:14

Did you know the meaning of these Biblical definitions?

1. Aaron – Bright
2. Abasement – degradation, humiliation
3. Abhor – To detest, loath, hate
4. Ability – Power to perform
5. Absalom – Father of peace
6. Admonition – Wise words spoken against evil
7. Adullam– Refuge
8. Adversity – Adverse circumstances caused by men's sin such as disobedience to God's law
9. Agag – Flaming or violent
10. Ambas age – An official commission coming to seek peace
11. Amnon – Faithful
12. Mocking – Imitating in fun or derision
13. Monarchy – The rule of one man

14. Morality – Principles of right conduct based on conscience comes from the heart
15. Muming – Sullen dissatisfaction with things
16. Mutability – Capable of change (physical world, social world)
17. Muting – Revolt against authority
18. Nepotism – Putting relatives in public office
19. Omnipotence – Infinite power
20. Onesimus – Useful
21. Oracle – A revelation
22. Owe – An obligation
23. Patricide – Murder of one's mother and father

KILLING BY SECRET AND SUDDEN ASSAULT

1. Eglon and Ehud   Judges 3:21
2. Sisera by Jael   Judges 4:17–21
3. Abner by Joab   2 Samuel 3:27
4. Ish-bosheth by sons   2 Samuel 4:5–8
5. Absolom   2 Samuel 13:28–29
6. Absolom by Joah   2 Samuel 18:14
7. Jehoram by Jehu   2 Kings 9:24
8. Jezebel by Jehu   2 Kings 9:30–37
9. Joash by servants   2 Kings 12:20–21
10. Zechariah by Shallum   2 Kings 15:10

Attempted cases:

1. Jacob by Esau   Genesis 27:41–45
2. Joseph by his brothers   Genesis 37:18–22
3. David by Saul   1 Samuel 15:10
4. Jesus by Jews   Luke 4:28–30, John 7:1
5. Paul by Jesus   Acts 1:23–25, Acts 23:12–31

Arts and Crafts in the Bible

1. Apothecary   Exodus 30:25, 25

2. Armorer   1 Samuel 8:12

3. Baker   Genesis 40:1

4. Barber   Ezekiel 5:1

5. Boat building   1 King 9:26

6. Brazier   Genesis 4:22

7. Brickmaker   Exodus 5:7

8. Calker   Ezekiel 27:9

9. Carpenter   Mark 6:3

10. Carver   Exodus 31:5

11. Confectioner   1 Samuel 13

12. Cook   1 Samuel 3:13

13. Coppersmith   2 Timothy 4:14

14. Draftsman   Ezekiel 4:1

15. Druggist   Exodus 30:25–35

16. Dyer   Exodus 25

17. Embalmer   Genesis 50:2, 3

18. Embroider   Exodus 35:35

19. Engrave   Exodus 28:35

20.	Fisherman	Matthew 4:18
21.	Founder	Judge 17: 4
22.	Fuller	Mark 9:3
23.	Gardener	John 20:15
24.	Goldsmith	Isaiah 40:19
25.	Husbandmen	Genesis 4:2
26.	Jeweler	John 25:17–21
27.	Lasidary	Exodus 27:8, 9
28.	Mariner	Ezekiel 27:89
29.	Moulderas	Exodus 32:4
30.	Mason	2 Samuel 5:11
31.	Musician	2 Samuel 6:5
32.	Needlework	Exodus 26:36
33.	Painting	Jeremiah 22:14
34.	Porter	2 Samuel 18:26
35.	Potter	Jeremiah 18:3
36.	Refiner	Malachi 3:2, 3
37.	Ropemaker	Judge 16:11
38.	Sewing	Ezekiel 13:18
39.	Silversmith	Acts 19:24
40.	Smelter	1 Samuel 13:19
41.	Smith	1 Samuel 13:19 Universal
42.	Stone cutter	Exodus 31, 5
43.	Tailor	Exodus 28:3, 4
44.	Tanner	Acts 10:6

45.	Tentmaking	Acts 18:3
46.	Weaver	John 19:23
47.	Winemaker	Nehemiah 13:15
48.	Workers in metal	Exodus 31:3
49.	Writers	Judges 5:14

AGRICULTURE

1. Fertilizing — The need to plant.
2. Grafting — Plowing the field Romans, 11:17–19.
3. Harrowing — Matthew 13:3, planting seeds in the ground.
4. Mowing — Clearing the field.
5. Pruning — Plowing and plows turning over earth for planting.
6. Reaping — Gathering the planted food.
7. Sowing — Into good soil.
8. Stacking — Taking something not yours.
9. Treading — Nehemiah 13:15, Judah some treading wine presses on the Sabbath.
10. Watering — 1 Corinthians 3:6–8, Man plants but God increases.
11. Weeding — Matthew 13:28–29; "Let both grow together until harvest" (Matthew 13:30).

⚜

SCRIPTURES RELATED TO SCIENCE

Science is the exact knowledge:

1. Architecture – Chronicles 2:1–18
2. Arithmetic – Matthew 18:22
3. Astronomy – Genesis 15:5
4. Biology – Psalm 139:13–16
5. Botany – 1 Kings 4:33
6. Chronology and history – 1 Chronicles 29:29
7. Geography – Genesis 10:1–30
8. Mechanics – Genesis 6:14–16, building of the ark
9. Medicine – Jeremiah 8:22
10. Meteorology – Job 38:24–26
11. Navigation – "They that go down to the sea in ships that do business in great waters" (Psalm 107:23).
12. Surveying – (Ezekiel 40:5)
13. Zoology – (1 Kings 4:33)
14. Astronauts

    Two men who traveled through space:

a. Enoch – He walked with God and he was not found. God took him (Genesis 5:22). By faith Enoch was told by God he would not see death (Hebrews 11:5).

b. Elijah – "And it come to pass as they still went on and talked, that behold, there appeared a chariot of fire, and horses of fire and parted them both, asunders and parted them both; and Elijah went up by a whirlwind into heaven" (2 Kings 2:11).

15. Pilot – When people think of a pilot, they always associate it with airlines; a pilot is one who guides.

ABOUT THE AUTHOR

Geraldine Smith has tried to be a peacemaker all her life. Matthew 5:9 says, "Blessed are the peacemakers for they shall called the children of God." She let her speech be seasoned with the grace of God so as not to offend anyone.

She was baptized in River Jordan. She was a missionary for ten years in Honduras.

Lord Jesus, let the words of my mouth and the meditation of my heart be acceptable in your sight. O Lord, my strength and my redeemer.